EVANGELINE
A Tale of Acadie

by

Henry Wadsworth Longfellow

NIMBUS
PUBLISHING

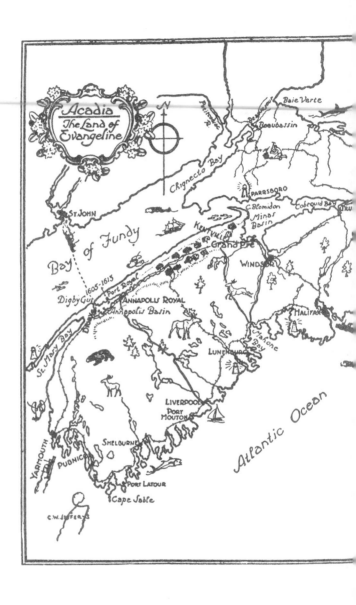

Acadia
The Land of Evangeline

N

Baie Verte

Petitcodiac R.

Beaubassin

Chignecto Bay

PARRSBORO

C. Blomidon

Cobequid Bay

TRU

Minas Basin

St. John

KENTVILLE

Bay of Fundy

Grand Pré

WINDSOR

1605-1613

Port Royal

Digby Gut

ANNAPOLIS ROYAL

Annapolis Basin

Digby

HALIFAX

Mahone Bay

St. Mary Bay

LUNENBURG

LIVERPOOL
Port Mouton

Atlantic Ocean

SHELBURNE

YARMOUTH

PUBNICO

Port Latour

Cape Sable

C. W. JEFFERYS

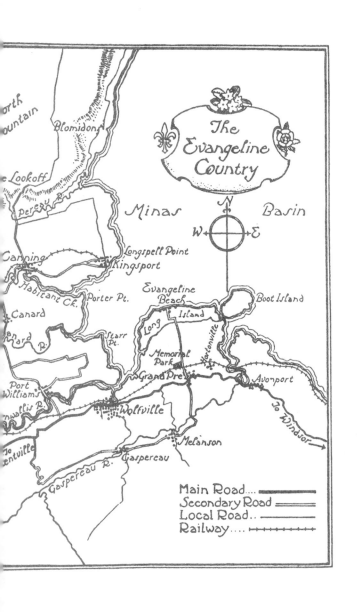

The Evangeline Country

North Mountain

Blomidon

Lookoff

Pereau R.

Minas Basin

N
W — E

Canning

Longspell Point
Kingsport

Habitant Ck.

Porter Pt.

Evangeline Beach

Boot Island

Canard

Long Island

Canard R.

Starr Pt.

Horton ville

Memorial Park

Port Williams

Grand Pré

Avonport

Cornwallis R.

Wolfville

To Windsor

To Kentville

Melanson

Gaspereau

Gaspereau R.

Main Road.... ━━━━━
Secondary Road ═══
Local Road.. ━━━
Railway.... ┼┼┼┼┼┼

Nimbus Publishing Limited
PO Box 9166
Halifax, NS   B3K 5M8
(902) 455-4286
www.nimbus.ca

Printed and bound in Canada
NB0995

Library and Archives Canada Cataloguing in Publication

      Longfellow, Henry Wadsworth, 1807-1882
      Evangeline : a tale of Acadie /
      Henry Wadsworth Longfellow.
      ISBN 978-1-77108-097-2

1. Acadians—Expulsion, 1755—Juvenile poetry. I. Title.
PS2263.A1 2013   j811'.3   C2013-901408-X

Nimbus Publishing acknowledges the financial support for its
publishing activities from the Government of Canada through the
Canada Book Fund (cbf) and the Canada Council for the Arts,
and from the Province of Nova Scotia through the Department of
Communities, Culture and Heritage.

The Genesis and Impact of *Evangeline*

Evangeline, A Tale of Acadie, the long romantic poem by Henry Wadsworth Longfellow, represents a milestone in the awakening of the collective consciousness of the Acadian people. Not only did Acadians identify with the story of Evangeline, but they saw their history acquire prestige and notoriety thanks to the international success of a work of fiction. By lifting Acadie out of the forgotten past, Longfellow honoured the courage and tenacity of the Acadian people.

How did an American poet who had never visited Nova Scotia become interested in the tragic story of the deportation (1755-1763) of the Acadians? Why did his epic poem capture the imagination of readers all over the world? Why did this poem have such a profound impact on the Acadian people?

Henry Wadsworth Longfellow was born on February 27, 1807, in Portland, Maine. He spent most of his youth in this quiet and charming town that inspired a number of his poems. When he was a young adolescent, he left for Bourdoin College, located about thirty miles from Portland. One of his classmates was Nathaniel Hawthorne, the future novelist who was to play a major role in the genesis of *Evangeline*.

After he graduated, Longfellow spent three years in Europe. He returned to the United States in 1829 to take a position at his alma mater, where he taught literarture for several years. In 1835, he and his wife decided to tour Europe. In the course of their travels, his wife took sick and died in Rotterdam. In 1836, Longfellow accepted a position as professor of modern languages at Harvard University in Cambridge, Massachusetts. During the seventeen years that he taught at Harvard, he continued to write poetry and translated a number of French and Spanish literary works.

In 1842, he left once again for Europe and remarried after he returned to Massachusetts. Several years after the publication of *Evangeline, A Tale of Acadie* in 1847, he resigned from his position at Harvard in order to devote himself exclusively to writing. The 1860s left Longfellow shattered by the events of the Civil War, the tragic death of his second wife and the death of his great friend Nathaniel Hawthorne. After another trip to Europe, where he was received with full honours, he returned to Cambridge where he spent the last twenty years of his life surrounded by friends. He died on May 24, 1882.

In order to understand the impact and cultural significance of the poem *Evangeline*, one should be aware of the historical events that led up to the deportation of the Acadians. Founded in 1604, but settled only after 1632, the French colony of Acadie covered the strategic territory that lay between New France (Quebec) and New England.

Unlike the huge French colony of New France, Acadie did not benefit from a French regime that flourished without interruption from 1608 to 1760. Not only did Acadie change hands on numerous occasions, but it was captured in 1710, fifty years before the fall of New France. According to the Treaty of Utrecht, signed in 1713 between France and Great Britain, France lost Acadie and Newfoundland, but kept Isle Royale (Cap Breton Island) et Isle Saint Jean (Prince Edward Island). The Acadians, who were Catholic and French-speaking, now found themselves in a Protestant and British colony that had been renamed Nova Scotia.

Under the terms of the Treaty of Utrecht, the Acadians were given a year to sign an oath of allegiance to the British monarch or to leave their fertile farms and settle on the French colony of Isle Royale. They refused to swear an unconditional oath of loyalty because they wanted to be guaranteed religious freedom and to be exempt from taking up arms against either the French or the Mi'kmaq in the event of war. After years of negotiations, the governor of Nova Scotia appeared to accept these conditions since the Acadians became known as the Neutrals or French Neutrals. The British authorities succeeded in convincing the majority of Acadian men to sign the oath of allegiance by promising them that they would not have to bear arms. In some cases, this promise was written in the margin of the French translation of the oath, and in other cases it was merely a verbal assurance.

Aside from the question of the oath of allegiance, the Acadians enjoyed a period of relative peace and prosperity that lasted until the late 1740s—a period which some historians call the Golden Age of Acadie. War broke ou once again between France and Great Britain in 1744. As a result, tensions grew in the colonies. The British built a fort in Piziquid (Windsor) and another one overlooking the marshes of Beaubassin (near the border of present-day New Brunswick and Nova Scotia). The following year, France countered by constructing Fort Beauséjour and Fort Gaspareau. The founding of Halifax in 1749 had also marked a turning point in the development of the colony of Nova Scotia. On the one hand, it established a solid British presence on the Atlantic coast mid-way between Boston and the large French fortress at Louisbourg on Isle Royale (Cape Breton Island). On the other hand, it constituted the first step in a systematic effort to colonize Nova Scotia with Protestant settlers who would eventually outnumber the French-speaking and Catholic Acadians.

In 1754, Charles Lawrence became lieutenant-governor of Nova Scotia. Like Governor William Shirley of Massachusetts, he had become increasingly suspicious of the Acadians' neutrality. Consequently he decided to take more aggressive measures. With the reinforcement of 2,000 volunteer troops from Massachusetts, Lieutenant-Colonel Robert Monckton captured the French forts at Beauséjour and Gaspareau.

Shortly after the fall of Fort Beauséjour, Captain Alexander Murray, who was stationed at Fort Edward in Piziquid, confiscated the guns and ammunition of the Acadians living in Grand-Pré, the most populated Acadian settlement. In July 1755, Lawrence ordered representatives of the various Acadian settlements to appear before the Council in Halifax in order to sign the unconditional oath of allegiance to the British Monarch. The delegates refused to sign the oath before consulting the inhabitants of their respective villages. As a result, they were imprisoned on George's Island in Halifax Harbour. On July 28, 1755, the Council in Halifax decided to proceed with the removal of the "French inhabitants" from the colony of Nova Scotia.

Although Grand-Pré has become the symbol of the expulsion of the Acadians, the deportation actually began at Fort Beauséjour (renamed Fort Cumberland) in August 1755. The inhabitants in the area were rounded up and imprisoned in the fort prior to being shipped to the British colonies along the eastern seaboard.

One month later, the deportation of the Acadians began at Grand-Pré. On September 5, Lieutenant-Colonel John Winslow, commander of the New England regiment stationed in the area, ordered the male inhabitants to assemble in the church Saint Charles des Mines. In other villages, the Acadians were informed that their lands, their houses and their livestock would be confiscated and that they and their families would be transported out of Nova Scotia. It is estimated that approximately 6,000 Acadians were deported from mainland Nova Scotia in 1755.

Although many Acadians perished on board the transport ships, the survivors were distributed in allotments to Massachusetts, Connecticut, New York, Pennsylvania, Maryland, Virginia, North Carolina, South Carolina and Georgia. Contrary to popular belief, no Acadians were actually deported from Nova Scotia to Louisiana since it was not a British colony.

After the fall of Louisbourg in 1758, the majority of Acadians living on Isle Royale and Isle Saint Jean were deported to England or France. Over a period of several years, the entire French-speaking population of the Atlantic region was thus shattered and dispersed. For the majority of the estimated 10,000 Acadians it meant deportation and life in exile, for others it meant a few years in hiding and for others almost fifty years of wandering.

In 1764, Acadians were given permission to resettle in Nova Scotia provided they took the oath of allegiance and settled in small groups in distant parts of the colony. As one of the darkest chapters in the history of Nova Scotia came to an end, the slow reconstruction of a people began.

When Henry Wadsworth Longfellow wrote his famous poem, there were only two historical works that described the deportation of the Acadians. One, published in 1770, was by Abbé Guillaume Raynal and the other, published in 1829, was by Thomas Chandler Haliburton. It is known that Longfellow borrowed a copy of Haliburton's book, *History of Nova Scotia*, from the library at Harvard on March 1841 and that he consulted *L'histoire philosophique et politique du commerce et des établissements des Européens dans les deux Indes* by Raynal. It was prior to that, however, that he was inspired to write a poem on the fate of the Acadians. Rev. Horace Lorenzo Conolly, an Anglican priest and friend of Nathaniel Hawthorne, had told him about two newlyweds who were separated by the deportation and how the young woman had wandered for years in search of her lover. She eventually found him, but he was on his death bed. The priest said a French-Canadian told him this tragic story about the young couple from Acadie. After listening to the story, Longfellow is reported to have said: "It is the best illustration of faithfulness and the constancy of a woman that I have ever heard or read." In 1845, he began writing his poetic version of the story. It was published two years later. Translated into many different languages, *Evangeline, A Tale of Acadie*, became an international bestseller.

The first edition of Pamphile Lemay's French translation of *Evangeline* was published in 1865 and, two years later, it appeared in serial form in the newspaper *Le Moniteur acadien*. In 1887, *L'Évangéline*, an Acadian newspaper named after Longfellow's heroine, also published the poem. By 1907, Acadian schoolchildren throughout the Maritime Provinces were reading extracts of the poem featured in one of their readers.

In the first part of the poem, Longfellow tells the story of two lovers, Gabriel Lajeunesse and Evangeline Bellefontaine, who grew up together in the beautiful village of Grand-Pré. Everything is perfect in this land of peace and plenty, an earthly paradise where pious Acadians work together in harmony. The engagement ceremony of the young lovers takes place under the watchful eye of the notary, René LeBlanc, and their fathers, Benedict and Basil. The following day, the engagement party is suddenly interrupted by the arrival of British soldiers and the sound of drums. The men and boys of the village are rounded up in the church where the commanding officer reads the order of deportation and informs them that their land, houses and livestock have been confiscated. Loaded onto British transport ships, the habitants of Grand-Pré watch as a wall of fire consumes their village. Evangeline and Gabriel are separated and their idyllic life comes to an end.

In the second part of the poem, we follow Evangeline as she wanders the continent in search of her beloved Gabriel. Her hope of finding him is renewed each time she encounters other exiled Acadians who assure her that he is not far off. She just misses him in the bayous of Louisiana. After years of wandering, Evangeline settles in Philadelphia where she works as a Sister of Mercy tending the sick and the poor. One day, in the middle of a smallpox epidemic, Evangeline finds Gabriel on his death bed in a hospital. He dies in her arms and shortly after, broken-hearted, she follows her fiancé to the grave.

⚜ ⚜ ⚜

Evangeline symbolizes loyalty, courage, piety and patience. These were important qualities for the

Acadian nationalists of the late nineteenth century who were attempting to unite Acadians scattered throughout Nova Scotia, New Brunswick and Prince Edward Island. Evangeline became a figurehead and source of inspiration that reinforced the feeling of belonging to a people. A similar phenomenon took place in Louisiana, where Evangeline also served to link Acadians of the south to Acadians of the north. In 1930, for example, Senator Dudley LeBlanc led a delegation of Evangelines to Canada. These young women visited various Acadian communities in Quebec, New Brunswick and Nova Scotia. Evangeline, the fictitious young woman from Grand-Pré immortalized by Longfellow, captured the imagination of Acadians for several generations.

After the construction of the railway in southeastern Nova Scotia in the 1870s, *Evangeline* also helped promote tourism. Thanks to the beauty of Longfellow's poetry and his emotionally appealing heroine, thousands of American tourists travelled to Nova Scotia looking for the "Land of Evangeline." In 1907, John Frederick Herbin, whose mother, Marie Robichaud, was an Acadian, bought an historically significant piece of land in Grand-Pré with the idea of developing a commemorative park dedicated to the memory of the Acadians. Ten years later, he sold the property to the Dominion Atlantic Railway, which erected the famous statue of Evangeline by the sculptors Philippe and Henri Hébert from Quebec. The Grand-Pré commemorative park became a national historic site in 1961.

Evangeline is a superb example of romantic poetry and a masterpiece of world literature. Longfellow was not the first author to provide an historical setting for a poignant love story. However, he brought the tragedy of the deportation of the Acadians to the attention of readers all over the world. Longfellow gave the Acadians an icon whose constancy in love and adversity still captivates our imagination.

Sally Ross & Barbara LeBlanc

References

Candow, James E. "The Deportation of the Acadians,"
booklet published by Environment Canada, Parks, 1986.

Fergusson, C. Bruce. "Introduction to *Evangeline, A Tale of
Acadie*." *Evangeline*. Halifax: Nimbus Publishing Limited,
1951.

Griffiths, Naomi. "Longfellow's *Evangeline*: The Birth and
Acceptance of a Legend." *Acadiensis*. Spring: 1982.

LeBlanc, Barbara. "*Evangeline* as Identity Myth." *Journal of
the Canadian Association of Ethnology and Folklore*. Vol. 15,
No. 2: 1993.

Maillet, Marguerite. *Histoire de la littérature acadienne*.
Moncton: Éditions d'Acadie, 1983.

Pellerin, Ginette. *Evangeline's Quest*. National Film Board of
Canada, 1996.

Ross, Sally and J. Alphonse Deveau. *The Acadians of Nova
Scotia*. Halifax: Nimbus Publishing, 1992.

Thériault, Léon. "Historical Synthesis, 1763-1990," in Jean
Daigle, ed., *Acadia of the Maritimes*. Chaire d'études
acadiennes: Université de Moncton, 1995.

EVANGELINE

A *Tale of Acadie*

Henry Wadsworth Longfellow

This is the forest primeval. The murmuring pines and the
hemlocks,
Bearded with moss, and in garments green, indistinct in the
twilight,
Stand like Druids of eld, with voices sad and prophetic,
Stand like harpers hoar, with beards that rest on their bosoms.
Loud from its rocky caverns, the deep-voiced neighbouring
ocean
Speaks, and in accents disconsolate answers the wail of the
forest.

*

This is the forest primeval; but where are the hearts that
beneath it
Leaped like the roe, when he hears in the woodland the voice
of the huntsman?
Where is the thatch-roofed village, the home of Acadian
farmers,—
Men whose lives glided on like rivers that water the
woodlands,
Darkened by shadows of earth, but reflecting an image of
heaven?
Waste are those pleasant farms, and the farmers forever
departed!

Scattered like dust and leaves, when the mighty blasts of
    October
Seize them, and whirl them aloft, and sprinkle them far o'er
    the ocean.
Naught but tradition remains of the beautiful village of
    Grand-Pré.
Ye who believe in affection that hopes, and endures, and is
    patient,
Ye who believe in the beauty and strength of woman's
    devotion,
List to the mournful tradition still sung by the pines of the
    forest;
List to a Tale of Love in Acadie, home of the happy.

PART THE FIRST

I

In the Acadian land, on the shores of the Basin of Minas,
Distant, secluded, still, the little village of Grand-Pré
Lay in the fruitful valley. Vast meadows stretched to the
eastward,
Giving the village its name, and pasture to flocks without
number.
Dikes, that the hands of the farmers had raised with labor
incessant,
Shut out the turbulent tides; but at stated seasons the flood-
gates
Opened, and welcomed the sea to wander at will o'er the
meadows.
West and south there were fields of flax, and orchards and
cornfields
Spreading afar and unfenced o'er the plain; and away to the
northward
Blomidon rose, and the forests old, and aloft on the mountains
Sea-fogs pitched their tents, and mists from the mighty
Atlantic
Looked on the happy valley, but ne'er from their station
descended.
There, in the midst of its farms, reposed the Acadian village.
Strongly built were the houses, with frames of oak and of
chestnut,
Such as the peasants of Normandy built in the reign of the
Henries.

Thatched were the roofs, with dormer-windows; and gables
    projecting
Over the basement below protected and shaded the door-way.
There in the tranquil evenings of summer, when brightly the
    sunset
Lighted the village street, and gilded the vanes on the
    chimneys,
Matrons and maidens sat in snow-white caps and in kirtles
Scarlet and blue and green, with distaffs spinning the golden
Flax for the gossiping looms, whose noisy shuttles within
    doors
Mingled their sound with the whir of the wheels and the
    songs of the maidens.
Solemnly down the street came the parish priest, and the
    children
Paused in their play to kiss the hand he extended to bless
    them.
Reverend walked he among them; and up rose matrons and
    maidens,
Hailing his slow approach with words of affectionate
    welcome.
Then came the laborers home from the field, and serenely the
    sun sank
Down to his rest, and twilight prevailed. Anon from the belfry
Softly the Angelus sounded, and over the roofs of the village
Columns of pale blue smoke, like clouds of incense
    ascending,
Rose from a hundred hearths, the homes of peace and
    contentment.
Thus dwelt together in love these simple Acadian farmers,—

Dwelt in the love of God and of man. Alike were they free from

Fear, that reigns with the tyrant, and envy, the vice of republics.

Neither locks had they to their doors, nor bars to their windows;

But their dwellings were open as day and the hearts of the owners;

There the richest was poor, and the poorest lived in abundance.

*

Somewhat apart from the village, and nearer the Basin of Minas,

Benedict Bellefontaine, the wealthiest farmer of Grand-Pré,

Dwelt on his goodly acres; and with him, directing his household,

Gentle Evangeline lived, his child, and the pride of the village.

Stalworth and stately in form was the man of seventy winters;

Hearty and hale was he, an oak that is covered with snow-flakes;

White as the snow were his locks, and his cheeks as brown as the oak-leaves.

Fair was she to behold, that maiden of seventeen summers.

Black were her eyes as the berry that grows on the thorn by the way-side,

Black, yet how softly they gleamed beneath the brown shade of her tresses!

Sweet was her breath as the breath of kine that feed in the meadows.

When in the harvest heat she bore to the reapers at noontide

Flagons of home-brewed ale, ah! fair in sooth was the maiden.

Fairer was she when, on Sunday morn, while the bell from its turret

Sprinkled with holy sounds the air, as the priest with his hyssop

Sprinkles the congregation, and scatters blessings upon them,

Down the long street she passed, with her chaplet of beads and her missal,

Wearing her Norman cap, and her kirtle of blue, and the ear-rings,

Brought in the olden time from France, and since, as an heirloom,

Handed down from mother to child, through long generations.

But a celestial brightness—a more ethereal beauty—

Shone on her face and encircled her form, when, after confession,

Homeward serenely she walked with God's benediction upon her.

When she had passed, it seemed like the ceasing of exquisite music.

Firmly builded with rafters of oak, the house of the farmer

Stood on the side of a hill commanding the sea; and a shady

Sycamore more grew by the door, with a woodbine wreathing around it.

Rudely carved was the porch, with seats beneath; and a footpath

Led through an orchard wide, and disappeared in the meadow.

Under the sycamore-tree were hives overhung by a penthouse,

Such as the traveller sees in regions remote by the road-side,

Built o'er a box for the poor, or the blessed image of Mary.

Farther down, on the slope of the hill, was the well with its moss-grown

Bucket, fastened with iron, and near it a trough for the horses.

Shielding the house from storms, on the north, were the barns and the farm-yard.

There stood the broad-wheeled wains and the antique ploughs and the harrows;

There were the folds for the sheep; and there, in his feathered seraglio,

Strutted the lordly turkey, and crowed the cock, with the selfsame

Voice that in ages of old had startled the penitent Peter.

Bursting with hay were the barns, themselves a village. In each one

Far o'er the gable projected a roof of thatch; and a staircase,

Under the sheltering eaves, led up to the odorous corn-loft.

There too the dove-cot stood, with its meek and innocent inmates

Murmuring ever of love; while above in the variant breezes

Numberless noisy weathercocks rattled and sang of mutation.

*

Thus, at peace with God and the world, the farmer of Grand-Pré

Lived on his sunny farm, and Evangeline governed his household.

Many a youth, as he knelt in church and opened his missal,

Fixed his eyes upon her, as the saint of his deepest devotion;

Happy was he who might touch her hand or the hem of her garment!

Many a suitor came to her door, by the darkness befriended,
And as he knocked and waited to hear the sound of her
    footsteps,
Knew not which beat the louder, his heart or the knocker of
    iron;
Or at the joyous feast of the Patron Saint of the village,
Bolder grew, and pressed her hand in the dance as he
    whispered
Hurried words of love, that seemed a part of the music.
But, among all who came, young Gabriel only was welcome;
Gabriel Lajeunesse, the son of Basil the blacksmith,
Who was a mighty man in the village, and honored of all men;
For since the birth of time, throughout all ages and nations,
Has the craft of the smith been held in repute by the people.
Basil was Benedict's friend. Their children from earliest
    childhood
Grew up together as brother and sister; and Father Felician,
Priest and pedagogue both in the village, had taught them
    their letters
Out of the selfsame book, with the hymns of the church and
    the plain-song.
But when the hymn was sung, and the daily lesson
    completed,
Swiftly they hurried away to the forge of Basil the blacksmith.
There at the door they stood, with wondering eyes to behold
    him
Take in his leathern lap the hoof of the horse as a plaything,
Nailing the shoe in its place; while near him the tire of the
    cart-wheel
Lay like a fiery snake, coiled round in a circle of cinders.

Oft on autumnal eves, when without in the gathering
	darkness

Bursting with light seemed the smithy, through every cranny
	and crevice,

Warm by the forge within they watched the laboring bellows,

And as its panting ceased, and the sparks expired in the ashes,

Merrily laughed, and said they were nuns going into the
	chapel.

Oft on sledges in winter, as swift as the swoop of the eagle,

Down the hill-side bounding, they glided away o'er the
	meadow.

Oft in the barns they climbed to the populous nests on the
	rafters,

Seeking with eager eyes that wondrous stone, which the
	swallow

Brings from the shore of the sea to restore the sight of its
	fledglings;

Lucky was he who found that stone in the nest of the
	swallow!

Thus passed a few swift years, and they no longer were
	children.

He was a valiant youth, and his face, like the face of the
	morning,

Gladdened the earth with its light, and ripened thought into
	action.

She was a woman now, with the heart and hopes of a woman.

"Sunshine of Saint Eulalie" was she called; for that was the
	sunshine

Which, as the farmers believed, would load their orchards
	with apples;

She, too, would bring to her husband's house delight and
   abundance,
Filling it full of love and the ruddy faces of children.

II

Now had the season returned, when the nights grow
   colder and longer,
And the retreating sun the sign of the Scorpion enters.
Birds of passage sailed through the leaden air, from the ice-
   bound,
Desolate northern bays to the shores of tropical islands.
Harvests were gathered in; and wild with the winds of
   September
Wrestled the trees of the forest, as Jacob of old with the angel.
All the signs foretold a winter long and inclement.
Bees, with prophetic instinct of want, had hoarded their
   honey
Till the hives overflowed; and the Indian hunters asserted
Cold would the winter be, for thick was the fur of the foxes.
Such was the advent of autumn. Then followed that beautiful
   season,
Called by the pious Acadian peasants the Summer of All-
   Saints!
Filled was the air with a dreamy and magical light; and the
   landscape
Lay as if new-created in all the freshness of childhood.
Peace seemed to reign upon earth, and the restless heart of
   the ocean

Was for a moment consoled. All sounds were in harmony blended.

Voices of children at play, the crowing of cocks in the farm-yards,

Whir of wings in the drowsy air, and the cooing of pigeons,

All were subdued and low as the murmurs of love, and the great sun

Looked with the eye of love through the golden vapors around him;

While arrayed in its robes of russet and scarlet and yellow,

Bright with the sheen of the dew, each glittering tree of the forest

Flashed like the plane-tree the Persian adorned with mantles and jewels.

*

Now recommenced the reign of rest and affection and stillness.

Day with its burden and heat had departed, and twilight descending

Brought back the evening star to the sky, and the herds to the homestead.

Pawing the ground they came, and resting their necks on each other,

And with their nostrils distended inhaling the freshness of evening.

Foremost, bearing the bell, Evangeline's beautiful heifer,

Proud of her snow-white hide, and the ribbon that waved from her collar,

Quietly paced and slow, as if conscious of human affection.

Then came the shepherd back with his bleating flocks from the sea-side,

Where was their favorite pasture. Behind them followed the
  watch-dog,
Patient, full of importance, and grand in the pride of his
  instinct,
Walking from side to side with a lordly air, and superbly
Waving his bushy tail, and urging forward the stragglers;
Regent of flocks was he when the shepherd slept; their
  protector,
When from the forest at night, through the starry silence, the
  wolves howled.
Late, with the rising moon, returned the wains from the
  marshes,
Laden with briny hay, that filled the air with its odor.
Cheerily neighed the steeds, with dew on their manes and
  their fetlocks,
While aloft on their shoulders the wooden and ponderous
  saddles,
Painted with brilliant dyes, and adorned with tassels of
  crimson,
Nodded in bright array, like hollyhocks heavy with blossoms.
Patiently stood the cows meanwhile, and yielded their udders
Unto the milkmaid's hand; whilst loud and in regular cadence
Into the sounding pail the foaming streamlets descended.
Lowing of cattle and peals of laughter were heard in the farm-
  yard,
Echoed back by the barns. Anon they sank into stillness;
Heavily closed, with a creaking sound, the valves of the barn-
  doors,
Rattled the wooden bars, and all for a season was silent.

*

In-doors, warm by the wide-mouthed fireplace, idly the farmer

Sat in his elbow-chair, and watched how the flames and the smoke-wreaths

Struggled together like foes in a burning city. Behind him,

Nodding and mocking along the wall, with gestures fantastic,

Darted his own huge shadow, and vanished away into darkness.

Faces, clumsily carved in oak, on the back of his arm-chair

Laughed in the flickering light, and the pewter plates on the dresser

Caught and reflected the flame, as shields of armies the sunshine.

Fragments of song the old man sang, and carols of Christmas,

Such as at home, in the olden time, his fathers before him

Sang in their Norman orchards and bright Burgundian vineyards.

Close at her father's side was the gentle Evangeline seated,

Spinning flax for the loom, that stood in the corner behind her.

Silent awhile were its treadles, at rest was its diligent shuttle,

While the monotonous drone of the wheel, like the drone of a bagpipe,

Followed the old man's song, and united the fragments together.

As in a church, when the chant of the choir at intervals ceases,

Footfalls are heard in the aisles, or words of the priest at the altar,

So, in each pause of the song, with measured motion the clock clicked.

*

Thus as they sat, there were footsteps heard, and, suddenly lifted,

Sounded the wooden latch, and the door swung back on its hinges.

Benedict knew by the hob-nailed shoes it was Basil the blacksmith,

And by her beating heart Evangeline knew who was with him.

"Welcome!" the farmer exclaimed, as their footsteps paused on the threshold,

"Welcome, Basil, my friend! Come, take thy place on the settle

Close by the chimney-side, which is always empty without thee;

Take from the shelf overhead thy pipe and the box of tobacco;

Never so much thyself art thou as when through the curling

Smoke of the pipe or the forge thy friendly and jovial face gleams

Round and red as the harvest moon through the midst of the marshes."

Then, with a smile of content, thus answered Basil the blacksmith,

Taking with easy air the accustomed seat by the fireside:—

"Benedict Bellefontaine, thou hast ever thy jest and thy ballad!

Ever in the cheerfullest mood art thou, when others are filled with

Gloomy forebodings of ill, and see only ruin before them.

Happy art thou, as if every day thou hadst picked up a horseshoe."

Pausing a moment, to take the pipe that Evangeline brought
him,

And with a coal from the embers had lighted, he slowly
continued:—

"Four days now are passed since the English ships at their
anchors

Ride in the Gaspereau's mouth, with their cannon pointed
against us.

What their design may be is unknown; but all are commanded

On the morrow to meet in the church, where his Majesty's
mandate

Will be proclaimed as law in the land. Alas! in the mean time

Many surmises of evil alarm the hearts of the people."

Then made answer the farmer:— "Perhaps some friendlier
purpose

Brings these ships to our shores. Perhaps the harvests in
England

By untimely rains or untimlier heat have been blighted,

And from our bursting barns they would feed their cattle and
children."

"Not so thinketh the folk in the village," said, warmly, the
blacksmith,

Shaking his head, as in doubt; then, heaving a sigh, he
continued:—

"Louisbourg is not forgotten, nor Beau Séjour, nor Port Royal.

Many already have fled to the forest, and lurk on its outskirts,

Waiting with anxious hearts the dubious fate of to-morrow.

Arms have been taken from us, and warlike weapons of all
kinds;

Nothing is left but the blacksmith's sledge and the scythe of
the mower."

Then with a pleasant smile made answer the jovial farmer:—

"Safer are we unarmed, in the midst of our flocks and our cornfields,

Safer within these peaceful dikes, beseiged by the ocean,

Than were our fathers in forts, beseiged by the enemy's cannon.

Fear no evil, my friend, and to-night may no shadow of sorrow

Fall on this house and hearth; for this is the night of the contract.

Built are the house and the barn. The merry lads of the village

Strongly have built them and well; and, breaking the glebe round about them,

Filled the barn with hay, and the house with food for a twelvemonth.

René Leblanc will be here anon, with his papers and inkhorn.

Shall we not then be glad, and rejoice in the joy of our children?"

As apart by the window she stood, with her hand in her lover's,

Blushing Evangeline heard the words that her father had spoken,

And as they died on his lips, the worthy notary entered.

III

Bent like a laboring oar, that toils in the surf of the ocean,
Bent, but not broken, by age was the form of the notary
public;

Shocks of yellow hair, like the silken floss of the maize, hung

Over his shoulders; his forehead was high; and glasses with
horn bows

Sat astride on his nose, with a look of wisdom supernal.

Father of twenty children was he, and more than a hundred

Children's children rode on his knee, and heard his great
watch tick.

Four long years in the times of the war had he languished a
captive,

Suffering much in an old French fort as the friend of the
English.

Now, though warier grown, without all guile or suspicion,

Ripe in wisdom was he, but patient, and simple, and
childlike.

He was beloved by all, and most of all by the children;

For he told them tales of the Loup-garou in the forest,

And of the goblin that came in the night to water the horses,

And of the white Létiche, the ghost of a child who
unchristened

Died, and was doomed to haunt unseen the chambers of
children;

And how on Christmas eve the oxen talked in the stable,

And how the fever was cured by a spider shut up in a
nutshell,

And of the marvellous powers of four-leaved clover and
     horseshoes,
With whatsoever else was writ in the lore of the village.
Then up rose from his seat by the fireside Basil the
     blacksmith,
Knocked from his pipe the ashes, and slowly extending his
     right hand,
"Father LeBlanc," he exclaimed, "thou hast heard the talk in
     the village,
And, perchance, canst tell us some news of these ships and
     their errand."
Then with modest demeanour made answer the notary
     public,—
"Gossip enough have I heard, in sooth, yet am never the
     wiser;
And what their errand may be I know not better than others.
Yet am I not of those who imagine some evil intention
Brings them here, for we are at peace; and why then molest
     us?"
"God's name!" shouted the hasty and somewhat irascible
     blacksmith;
"Must we in all things look for the how, and the why, and the
     wherefore?
Daily injustice is done, and might is the right of the
     strongest!"
But, without heeding his warmth, continued the notary
     public,—
"Man is unjust, but God is just; and finally justice
Triumphs; and well I remember a story, that often consoled
     me,
When as a captive I lay in the old French fort at Port Royal."

This was the old man's favorite tale, and he loved to repeat it

Whenever neighbours complained that any injustice was done
them.

"Once in an ancient city, whose name I no longer remember,

Raised aloft on a column, a brazen statue of Justice

Stood in the public square, upholding the scales in its left
hand,

And in its right a sword, as an emblem that justice presided

Over the laws of the land, and the hearts and homes of the
people.

Even the birds had built their nests in the scales of the
balance,

Having no fear of the sword that flashed in the sunshine
above them.

But in the course of time the laws of the land were corrupted;

Might took the place of right, and the weak were oppressed,
and the mighty

Ruled with an iron rod. Then it chanced in a nobleman's
palace

That a necklace of pearls was lost, and ere long a suspicion

Fell on an orphan girl who lived as a maid in the household.

She, after form of trial condemned to die on the scaffold,

Patiently met her doom at the foot of the statue of Justice.

As to her Father in Heaven her innocent spirit ascended,

Lo! o'er the city a tempest rose; and the bolts of the thunder

Smote the statue of bronze, and hurled in wrath from its left
hand

Down on the pavement below the clattering scales of the
balance,

And in the hollow thereof was found the nest of a magpie,

Into whose clay-built walls the necklace of pearls was
    inwoven."

Silenced, but not convinced, when the story was ended, the
    blacksmith

Stood like a man who fain would speak, but findeth no
    language;

And all his thoughts were congealed into lines on his face, as
    the vapors

Freeze in fantastic shapes on the window-panes in the winter.

*

Then Evangeline lighted the brazen lamp on the table,

Filled, till it overflowed, the pewter tankard with home-
    brewed

Nut-brown ale, that was famed for its strength in the village
    of Grand-Pré;

While from his pocket the notary drew his papers and ink-
    horn,

Wrote with a steady hand the date and the age of the parties,

Naming the dower of the bride in flocks of sheep and in
    cattle.

Orderly all things proceeded, and duly and well were
    completed,

And the great seal of the law was set like a sun on the margin.

Then from his leathern pouch the farmer threw on the table

Three times the old man's fee in solid pieces of silver;

And the notary rising, and blessing the bride and the
    bridegroom,

Lifted aloft the tankard of ale and drank to their welfare.

Wiping the foam from his lip, he solemnly bowed and
    departed,

While in silence the others sat and mused by the fireside,

Till Evangeline brought the draught-board out of its corner.

Soon was the game begun. In friendly contention the old men

Laughed at each lucky hit, or unsuccessful manoeuvre,

Laughed when a man was crowned, or a breach was made in
the king-row.

Meanwhile apart, in the twilight gloom of a window's
embrasure,

Sat the lovers, and whispered together, beholding the moon
rise

Over the pallid sea and the silvery mist of the meadows.

Silently one by one, in the infinite meadows of heaven,

Blossomed the lovely stars, the forget-me-nots of the angels.

*

Thus passed the evening away. Anon the bell from the belfry

Rang out the hour of nine, the village curfew, and straightway

Rose the guests and departed; and silence reigned in the
household.

Many a farewell word and sweet good-night on the door-step

Lingered long in Evangeline's heart, and filled it with
gladness.

Carefully then were covered the embers that glowed on the
hearth-stone,

And on the oaken stairs resounded the tread of the farmer.

Soon with a soundless step the foot of Evangeline followed.

Up the staircase moved a luminous space in the darkness,

Lighted less by lamp than the shining face of the maiden.

Silent she passed through the hall, and entered the door of
her chamber.

Simple that chamber was, with its curtains of white, and its
clothes-press

Ample and high, on whose spacious shelves were carefully
   folded

Linen and woollen stuffs, by the hand of Evangeline woven.

This was the precious dower she would bring to her husband
   in marriage,

Better than flocks and herds, being proofs of her skill as a
   housewife.

Soon she extinguished her lamp, for the mellow and radiant
   moonlight

Streamed through the windows, and lighted the room, till the
   heart of the maiden

Swelled and obeyed its power, like the tremulous tides of the
   ocean.

Ah! she was fair, exceeding fair to behold, as she stood with

Naked snow-white feet on the gleaming floor of her chamber!

Little she dreamed that below, among the trees of the
   orchard,

Waited her lover and watched for the gleam of her lamp and
   her shadow.

Yet were her thoughts of him, and at times a feeling of
   sadness

Passed o'er her soul, as the sailing shade of clouds in the
   moonlight

Flitted across the floor and darkened the room for a moment.

And as she gazed from the window, she saw serenely the
   moon pass

Forth from the folds of a cloud, and one star follow her
   footsteps,

As out of Abraham's tent young Ishmael wandered with
   Hagar!

IV

Pleasantly rose next morn the sun on the village of Grand-Pré.

Pleasantly gleamed in the soft, sweet air the Basin of Minas,

Where the ships, with their wavering shadows, were riding at anchor.

Life had long been astir in the village, and clamorous labor

Knocked with its hundred hands at the golden gates of the morning.

Now from the country around, from the farms and neighbouring hamlets,

Came in their holiday dresses the blithe Acadian peasants.

Many a glad good-morrow and jocund laugh from the young folk

Made the bright air brighter, as up from the numerous meadows,

Where no path could be seen but the track of wheels in the greensward,

Group after group appeared, and joined, or passing on the highway.

Long ere noon, in the village all sounds of labor were silenced.

Thronged were the streets with people; and noisy groups at the house-doors

Sat in the cheerful sun, and rejoiced and gossiped together.

Every house was an inn, where all were welcomed and feasted;

For with this simple people, who lived like brothers together,

All things were held in common, and what one had was
    another's.

Yet under Benedict's roof hospitality seemed more abundant:

For Evangeline stood among the guests of her father;

Bright was her face with smiles, and words of welcome and
    gladness

Fell from her beautiful lips, and blessed the cup as she gave it.

*

Under the open sky, in the odorous air of the orchard,

Bending with golden fruit, was spread the feast of betrothal.

There in the shade of the porch were the priest and the
    notary seated;

There good Benedict sat, and sturdy Basil the blacksmith.

Not far withdrawn from these, by the cider-press and the
    beehives,

Michael the fiddler was placed, with the gayest of hearts and
    of waistcoats.

Shadow and light from the leaves alternately played on his
    snow-white

Hair, as it waved in the wind; and the jolly face of the fiddler

Glowed like a living coal when the ashes are blown from the
    embers.

Gayly the old man sang to the vibrant sound of his fiddle,

Tous les Bourgeois de Chartres, and Le Carillon de
    Dunkerque.

And anon with his wooden shoes beat time to the music.

Merrily, merrily whirled the wheels of the dizzying dances

Under the orchard-trees and down the path to the meadows;

Old folk and young together, and children mingled among
    them.

Fairest of all the maids was Evangeline, Benedict's daughter!

Noblest of all the youths was Gabriel, son of the blacksmith!

*

So passed the morning away. And lo! with a summons sonorous

Sounded the bell from its tower, and over the meadows a drum beat.

Thronged ere long was the church with men. Without, in the churchyard,

Waited the women. They stood by the graves, and hung on the head-stones

Garlands of autumn-leaves and evergreens fresh from the forest.

Then came the guard from the ships, and marching proudly among them

Entered the sacred portal. With loud and dissonant clangor

Echoed the sound of their brazen drums from ceiling and casement,—

Echoed a moment only, and slowly the ponderous portal

Closed, and in silence the crowd awaited the will of the soldiers.

Then uprose their commander, and spake from the steps of the altar,

Holding aloft in his hands, with its seals, the royal commission.

"You are convened this day," he said, "by his Majesty's orders.

Clement and kind has he been; but how you have answered his kindness,

Let your own hearts reply! To my natural make and my temper

Painful the task is I do, which to you I know must be grievous.

Yet must I bow and obey, and deliver the will of our monarch;

Namely, that all your lands, and dwellings, and cattle of all
kinds

Forfeited be to the crown; and that you yourselves from this
province

Be transported to other lands. God grant you may dwell there

Ever as faithful subjects, a happy and peaceable people!

Prisoners now I declare you; for such is his Majesty's
pleasure!"

As, when the air is serene in the sultry solstice of summer,

Suddenly gathers a storm, and the deadly sling of the
hailstones

Beats down the farmer's corn in the field and shatters his
windows,

Hiding the sun, and strewing the ground with thatch from the
house-roofs,

Bellowing fly the herds, and seek to break their inclosures;

So on the hearts of the people descended the words of the
speaker.

Silent a moment they stood in speechless wonder, and then
rose

Louder and ever louder a wail of sorrow and anger,

And, by one impulse moved, they madly rushed to the door-
way.

Vain was the hope of escape; and cries and fierce imprecations

Rang through the house of prayer; and high o'er the heads of
the others

Rose, with his arms uplifted, the figure of Basil the
blacksmith,

As, on a stormy sea, a spar is tossed by the billows.

Flushed was his face and distorted with passion; and wildly he
   shouted,—

"Down with the tyrants of England! we never have sworn
   them allegiance!

Death to these foreign soldiers, who seize on our homes and
   our harvests!"

More he fain would have said, but the merciless hand of a
   soldier

Smote him upon the mouth, and dragged him down to the
   pavement.

*

In the midst of the strife and tumult of angry contention,

Lo! the door of the chancel opened, and Father Felician

Entered, with serious mien, and ascended the steps of the
   altar.

Raising his reverend hand, with a gesture he awed into silence

All that clamorous throng; and thus he spake to his people;

Deep were his tones and solemn; in accents measured and
   mournful

Spake he, as, after the tocsin's alarum, distinctly the clock
   strikes.

"What is this that ye do, my children? what madness has seized
   you?

Forty years of my life have I labored among you, and taught
   you,

Not in word alone, but in deed, to love one another!

Is this the fruit of my toils, of my vigils and prayers and
   privations?

Have you so soon forgotten all lessons of love and forgiveness?

This is the house of the Prince of Peace, and would you
   profane it

Thus with violent deeds and hearts overflowing with hatred?

Lo! where the crucified Christ from His cross is gazing upon you!

See! in those sorrowful eyes what meekness and holy compassion!

Hark! how those lips still repeat the prayer, 'O Father, forgive them!'

Let us repeat that prayer in the hour when the wicked assail us,

Let us repeat it now, and say, 'O Father, forgive them!'"

Few were his words of rebuke, but deep in the hearts of his people

Sank they, and sobs of contrition succeeded that passionate outbreak;

And they repeated his prayer, and said, "O Father, forgive them!"

*

Then came the evening service. The tapers gleamed from the altar.

Fervent and deep was the voice of the priest, and the people responded,

Not with their lips alone, but their hearts; and the Ave Maria

Sang they, and fell on their knees, and their souls, with devotion translated,

Rose on the ardor of prayer, like Elijah ascending to heaven.

*

Meanwhile had spread in the village the tidings of ill, and on all sides

Wandered, wailing, from house to house the women and children.

Long at her father's door Evangeline stood, with her right hand

Shielding her eyes from the level rays of the sun, that, descending,

Lighted the village street with mysterious splendor, and roofed each

Peasant's cottage with golden thatch, and emblazoned its windows.

Long within had been spread the snow-white cloth on the table;

There stood the wheaten loaf, and the honey fragrant with wild flowers;

There stood the tankard of ale, and the cheese fresh brought from the dairy;

And at the head of the board, the great arm-chair of the farmer.

Thus did Evangeline wait at her father's door, as the sunset

Threw the long shadows of trees o'er the broad ambrosial meadows.

Ah! on her spirit within a deeper shadow had fallen,

And from the fields of her soul a fragrance celestial ascended,—

Charity, meekness, love, and hope, and forgiveness, and patience!

Then, all-forgetful of self, she wandered into the village,

Cheering with looks and words the disconsolate hearts of the women,

As o'er the darkening fields with lingering steps they departed,

Urged by their household cares, and the weary feet of their children.

Down sank the great red sun, and in golden, glimmering vapors

Veiled the light of his face, like the Prophet descending from
Sinai.

Sweetly over the village the bell of the Angelus sounded.

*

Meanwhile, amid the gloom, by the church Evangeline
lingered.

All was silent within; and in vain at the door and the windows

Stood she, and listened and looked, until, overcome by
emotion,

"Gabriel!" cried she aloud with tremulous voice; but no answer

Came from the graves of the dead, nor the gloomier grave of
the living.

Slowly at length she returned to the tenantless house of her
father.

Smouldered the fire on the hearth, on the board was the
supper untasted,

Empty and drear was each room, and haunted with phantoms
of terror.

Sadly echoed her step on the stair and the floor of her
chamber.

In the dead of the night she heard the whispering rain fall

Loud on the withered leaves of the sycamore-tree by the
window.

Keenly the lightning flashed; and the voice of the
neighbouring thunder

Told her that God was in heaven, and governed the world he
created!

Then she remembered the tale she had heard of the justice of
Heaven;

Soothed was her troubled soul, and she peacefully slumbered
till morning.

V

Four times the sun had risen and set; and now on the fifth day

Cheerily called the cock to the sleeping maids of the farm-house.

Soon o'er the yellow fields, in silent and mournful procession,

Came from the neighbouring hamlets and farms the Acadian women,

Driving in ponderous wains their household goods to the sea-shore,

Pausing and looking back to gaze once more on their dwellings,

Ere they were shut from sight by the winding road and the woodland.

Close at their sides their children ran, and urged on the oxen,

While in their little hands they clasped some fragments of playthings.

*

Thus, to the Gaspereau's mouth they hurried; and there on the sea-beach

Piled in confusion lay the household goods of the peasants.

All day long between the shore and the ships did the boats ply;

All day long the wains came laboring down from the village.

Late in the afternoon, when the sun was near to his setting,

Echoed far o'er the fields came the roll of drums from the church-yard.

Thither the women and children thronged. On a sudden the church-doors

Opened, and forth came the guard, and marching in gloomy
    procession

Followed the long-imprisoned, but patient, Acadian farmers.

Even as pilgrims, who journey afar from their homes and their
    country,

Sing as they go, and in singing forget they are weary and way-
    worn,

So with songs on their lips the Acadian peasants descended

Down from the church to the shore, amid their wives and
    their daughters.

Foremost the young men came; and, raising together their
    voices,

Sang they with tremulous lips a chant of the Catholic
    Missions:—

"Sacred heart of the Saviour! O inexhaustible fountain!

Fill our hearts this day with strength and submission and
    patience!"

Then the old men, as they marched, and the women that
    stood by the way-side

Joined in the sacred psalm, and the birds in the sunshine
    above them

Mingled their notes therewith, like voices of spirits departed.

*

Half-way down to the shore Evangeline waited in silence,

Not overcome with grief, but strong in the hour of affliction,—

Calmly and sadly she waited, until the procession approached
    her,

And she beheld the face of Gabriel pale with emotion.

Tears then filled her eyes, and, eagerly running to meet him,

Clasped she his hands, and laid her head on his shoulder, and
    whispered,—

"Gabriel! be of good cheer! for if we love one another,

Nothing, in truth, can harm us, whatever mischances may
happen!"

Smiling she spake these words; then suddenly paused, for her
father

Saw she slowly advancing. Alas! how changed was his aspect!

Gone was the glow from his cheek, and the fire from his eye,
and his footstep

Heavier seemed with the weight of the heavy heart in his
bosom.

But with a smile and a sigh, she clasped his neck and
embraced him,

Speaking words of endearment where words of comfort
availed not.

Thus to the Gaspereau's mouth moved on that mournful
procession.

*

There disorder prevailed, and the tumult and stir of
embarking.

Busily plied the freighted boats; and in the confusion

Wives were torn from their husbands, and mothers, too late,
saw their children

Left on the land, extending their arms, with wildest
entreaties.

So unto separate ships were Basil and Gabriel carried,

While in despair on the shore Evangeline stood with her
father.

Half the task was not done when the sun went down, and the
twilight

Deepened and darkened around; and in haste the refluent
ocean

Fled away from the shore, and left the line of the sand-beach
Covered with waifs of the tide, with kelp and the slippery
sea-weed.
Farther back in the midst of the household goods and the
wagons,
Like to a gypsy camp, or a leaguer after a battle,
All escape cut off by the sea, and the sentinels near them,
Lay encamped for the night the houseless Acadian farmers.
Back to its nethermost caves retreated the bellowing ocean,
Dragging adown the beach the rattling pebbles, and leaving
Inland and far up the shore the stranded boats of the sailors.
Then, as the night descended, the herds returned from their
pastures;
Sweet was the moist still air with the odor of milk from their
udders;
Lowing they waited, and long, at the well-known bars of the
farm-yard,—
Waited and looked in vain for the voice and the hand of the
milkmaid.
Silence reigned in the street; from the church no Angelus
sounded,
Rose no smoke from the roofs, and gleamed no lights from
the windows.

*

But on the shores meanwhile the evening fires had been
kindled,
Built of the drift-wood thrown on the sands from wrecks in
the tempest.
Round them shapes of gloom and sorrowful faces were
gathered,

Voices of women were heard, and of men, and the crying of children.

Onward from fire to fire, as from hearth to hearth in his parish,

Wandered the faithful priest, consoling and blessing and cheering,

Like unto shipwrecked Paul on Melita's desolate sea-shore.

Thus he approached the place where Evangeline sat with her father,

And in the flickering light beheld the face of the old man,

Haggard and hollow and wan, and without either thought or emotion.

E'en as the face of a clock from which the hands have been taken.

Vainly Evangeline strove with words and caresses to cheer him,

Vainly offered him food; yet he moved not, he looked not, he spake not,

But, with a vacant stare, ever gazed at the flickering fire-light.

"Benedicite!" murmured the priest, in tones of compassion.

More he fain would have said, but his heart was full, and his accents

Faltered and paused on his lips, as the feet of a child on a threshold,

Hushed by the scene he beholds, and the awful presence of sorrow.

Silently, therefore, he laid his hand on the head of the maiden,

Raising his eyes, full of tears, to the silent stars that above them

Moved on their way, unperturbed by the wrongs and sorrows of mortals.

Then sat he down at her side, and they wept together in
    silence.

*

Suddenly rose from the south a light, as in autumn the blood-
    red
Moon climbs the crystal walls of heaven, and o'er the horizon
Titan-like stretches its hundred hands upon mountain and
    meadow,
Seizing the rocks and the rivers, and piling huge shadows
    together.
Broader and ever broader it gleamed on the roofs of the
    village,
Gleamed on the sky and the sea, and the ships that lay in the
    roadstead.
Columns of shining smoke uprose, and flashes of flame were
Thrust through their folds and withdrawn, like the quivering
    hands of a martyr.
Then as the winds seized the gleeds and the burning thatch,
    and, uplifting,
Whirled them aloft through the air, at once from a hundred
    house-tops
Started the sheeted smoke with flashes of flame intermingled.

*

These things beheld in dismay the crowd on the shore and on
    shipboard.
Speechless at first they stood, then cried aloud in their
    anguish,
"We shall behold no more our homes in the village of Grand-
    Pré!"
Loud on a sudden the cocks began to crow in the farm-yards,
Thinking the day had dawned; and anon the lowing of cattle

Came on the evening breeze, by the barking of dogs
    interrupted.

Then rose the sound of dread, such as startles the sleeping
    encampments

Far in the western prairies or forests that skirt the Nebraska,

When the wild horses affrighted sweep by with the speed of
    the whirlwind,

Or the loud bellowing herds of buffaloes rush to the river.

Such was the sound that arose on the night, as the herds and
    the horses

Broke through their folds and fences, and madly rushed o'er
    the meadows.

*

Overwhelmed with the sight, yet speechless, the priest and
    the maiden

Gazed on the scene of terror that reddened and widened
    before them;

And as they turned at length to speak to their silent
    companion,

Lo! from his seat he had fallen, and stretched abroad on the
    sea-shore

Motionless lay his form, from which the soul had departed.

Slowly the priest uplifted the lifeless head, and the maiden

Knelt at her father's side, and wailed aloud in her terror.

Then in a swoon she sank, and lay with her head on his
    bosom.

Through the long night she lay in deep, oblivious slumber;

And when she awoke from the trance, she beheld a multitude
    near her.

Faces of friends she beheld, that were mournfully gazing
    upon her,

Pallid, with tearful eyes, and looks of saddest compassion.
Still the blaze of the burning village illumined the landscape,
Reddened the sky overhead, and gleamed on the faces
    around her,
And like the day of doom it seemed to her wavering senses.
Then a familiar voice she heard, as it said to the people,—
"Let us bury him here by the sea. When a happier season
Brings us again to our homes from the unknown land of our
    exile,
Then shall his sacred dust be piously laid in the church-yard."
Such were the words of the priest. And there in haste by the
    sea-side,
Having the glare of the burning village for funeral torches,
But without bell or book, they buried the farmer of Grand-
    Pré.
And as the voice of the priest repeated the service of sorrow,
Lo! with a mournful sound, like the voice of a vast
    congregation,
Solemnly answered the sea, and mingled its roar with the
    dirges.
'T was the returning tide, that afar from the waste of the
    ocean,
With the first dawn of the day, came heaving and hurrying
    landward.
They recommenced once more the stir and noise of
    embarking;
And with the ebb of that tide the ships sailed out of the
    harbour,
Leaving behind them the dead on the shore, and the village
    in ruins.

PART THE SECOND

I

M any a weary year had passed since the burning of
Grand-Pré,

When on the falling tide the freighted vessels departed,

Bearing a nation, with all its household gods, into exile,

Exile without an end, and without an example in story.

Far asunder, on separate coasts, the Acadians landed;

Scattered were they, like flakes of snow, when the wind from
the northeast

Strikes aslant through the fogs that darken the Banks of
Newfoundland.

Friendless, homeless, hopeless, they wandered from city to
city,

From the cold lakes of the North to sultry Southern
savannas,—

From the bleak shores of the sea to the lands where the
Father of Waters

Seizes the hills in his hands, and drags them down to the
ocean,

Deep in their sands to bury the scattered bones of the
mammoth.

Friends they sought and homes; and many, despairing, heart-
broken,

Asked of the earth but a grave, and no longer a friend nor a
fireside.

Written their history stands on tablets of stone in the church-
yards.

Long among them was seen a maiden who waited and
wandered,

Lowly and meek in spirit, and patiently suffering all things.

Fair was she and young; but, alas! before her extended,

Dreary and vast and silent, the desert of life, with its pathway

Marked by the graves of those who had sorrowed and suffered
before her,

Passions long extinguished, and hopes long dead and
abandoned,

As the emigrant's way o'er the Western desert is marked by

Camp-fires long consumed, and bones that bleach in the
sunshine.

Something there was in her life incomplete, imperfect,
unfinished;

As if a morning of June, with all its music and sunshine,

Suddenly paused in the sky, and, fading, slowly descended

Into the east again, from whence it late had arisen.

Sometimes she lingered in towns, till, urged by the fever
within her,

Urged by a restless longing, the hunger and thirst of the spirit,

She would commence again her endless search and endeavour;

Sometimes in church-yards strayed, and gazed on the crosses
and tombstones,

Sat by some nameless grave, and thought that perhaps in its
bosom

He was already at rest, and she longed to slumber beside him.

Sometimes a rumor, a hearsay, an inarticulate whisper,

Came with its airy hand to point and beckon her forward.

Sometimes she spake with those who had seen her beloved
and known him,

But it was long ago, in some far-off place or forgotten.

"Gabriel Lajeunesse!" they said; "Oh yes! we have seen him.

He was with Basil the blacksmith, and both have gone to the prairies;

Coureurs-des-Bois are they, and famous hunters and trappers."

"Gabriel Lajeunesse!" said others; "Oh yes! we have seen him.

He is a Voyageur in the lowlands of Louisiana."

Then they would say,—"Dear child! why dream and wait for him longer?

Are there not other youths as fair as Gabriel? others

Who have hearts as tender and true, and spirits as loyal?

Here is Baptiste Leblanc, the notary's son, who has loved thee

Many a tedious year; come, give him thy hand and be happy!

Thou art too fair to be left to braid St. Catherine's tresses."

Then would Evangeline answer, serenely but sadly,—"I cannot!

Whither my heart has gone, there follows my hand, and not elsewhere.

For when the heart goes before, like a lamp, and illumines the pathway,

Many things are made clear, that else lie hidden in darkness."

Thereupon the priest, her friend and father-confessor,

Said, with a smile,—"O daughter! thy God thus speaketh within thee!

Talk not of wasted affection, affection never was wasted;

If it enrich not the heart of another, its waters, returning

Back to their springs, like the rain, shall fill them full of refreshment;

That which the fountain sends forth returns again to the fountain.

Patience; accomplish thy labor; accomplish thy work of affection!

Sorrow and silence are strong, and patient endurance is godlike.

Therefore accomplish thy labor of love, till the heart is made godlike,

Purified, strengthened, perfected, and rendered more worthy of heaven!"

Cheered by the good man's words, Evangeline labored and waited.

Still in her heart she heard the funeral dirge of the ocean,

But with its sound there was mingled a voice that whispered, "Despair not!"

Thus did that poor soul wander in want and cheerless discomfort,

Bleeding, barefooted, over the shards and thorns of existence.

Let me essay, O Muse! to follow the wanderer's footsteps;—

Not through each devious path, each changeful year of existence;

But as a traveller follows a streamlet's course through the valley:

Far from its margin at times, and seeing the gleam of its water

Here and there, in some open space, and at intervals only;

Then drawing nearer its banks, through sylvan glooms that conceal it,

Though he behold it not, he can hear its continuous murmur;

Happy, at length, if he find the spot where it reaches an outlet.

II

It was the month of May. Far down the Beautiful River,
Past the Ohio shore and past the mouth of the Wabash,
Into the golden stream of the broad and swift Mississippi,
Floated a cumbrous boat, that was rowed by Acadian boatmen.
It was a band of exiles: a raft, as it were, from the shipwrecked
Nation, scattered along the coast, now floating together,
Bound by the bonds of a common belief and a common
    misfortune;
Men and women and children, who, guided by hope or by
    hearsay,
Sought for their kith and their kin among the few-acred
    farmers
On the Acadian coast, and the prairies of fair Opelousas.
With them Evangeline went, and her guide, the Father
    Felician.
Onward o'er sunken sands, through a wilderness sombre with
    forests,
Day after day they glided adown the turbulent river;
Night after night, by their blazing fires, encamped on its
    borders.
Now through rushing chutes, among green islands, where
    plumelike
Cotton-trees nodded their shadowy crests, they swept with
    the current,
Then emerged into broad lagoons, where silvery sand-bars
Lay in the stream, and along the wimpling waves of their
    margin,

Shining with snow-white plumes, large flocks of pelicans
    waded.

Level the landscape grew, and along the shores of the river,

Shaded by china-trees, in the midst of luxuriant gardens,

Stood the houses of planters, with negro-cabins and dove-
    cots.

They were approaching the region where reigns perpetual
    summer,

Where through the Golden Coast, and groves of orange and
    citron,

Sweeps with majestic curve the river away to the eastward.

They, too, swerved from their course; and, entering the Bayou
    of Plaquemine,

Soon were lost in a maze of sluggish and devious waters,

Which, like a network of steel, extended in every direction.

Over their heads the towering and tenebrous boughs of the
    cypress

Met in a dusky arch, and trailing mosses in mid air

Waved like banners that hang on the walls of ancient
    cathedrals.

Deathlike the silence seemed, and unbroken, save by the
    herons

Home to their roosts in the cedar-trees returning at sunset,

Or by the owl, as he greeted the moon with demoniac
    laughter.

Lovely the moonlight was as it glanced and gleamed on the
    water,

Gleamed on the columns of cypress and cedar sustaining the
    arches,

Down through whose broken vaults it fell as through chinks
    in a ruin.

Dreamlike, and indistinct, and strange were all things around
    them;

And o'er their spirits there came a feeling of wonder and
    sadness,—

Strange forebodings of ill, unseen and that cannot be
    compassed.

As, at the tramp of a horse's hoof on the turf of the prairies,

Far in advance are closed the leaves of the shrinking mimosa,

So, at the hoof-beats of fate, with sad forebodings of evil,

Shrinks and closes the heart, ere the stroke of doom has
    attained it.

But Evangeline's heart was sustained by a vision, that faintly

Floated before her eyes, and beckoned her on through the
    moonlight.

It was the thought of her brain that assumed the shape of a
    phantom.

Through those shadowy aisles had Gabriel wandered before
    her,

And every stroke of the oar now brought him nearer and
    nearer.

*

Then in his place, at the prow of the boat, rose one of the
    oarsmen,

And, as a signal sound, if others like them peradventure

Sailed on those gloomy and midnight streams, blew a blast on
    his bugle.

Wild through the dark colonnades and corridors leafy the blast
    rang,

Breaking the seal of silence, and giving tongues to the forest.

Soundless above them the banners of moss just stirred to the
    music.

Multitudinous echoes awoke and died in the distance,

Over the watery floor, and beneath the reverberant branches;

But not a voice replied; no answer came from the darkness;

And when the echoes had ceased, like a sense of pain was the silence.

Then Evangeline slept; but the boatmen rowed through the midnight,

Silent at times, then singing familiar Canadian boat-songs,

Such as they sang of old on their own Acadian rivers.

And through the night were heard the mysterious sounds of the desert,

Far off, indistinct, as of wave or wind in the forest,

Mixed with the whoop of the crane and the roar of the grim alligator.

*

Thus ere another noon they emerged from those shades; and before them

Lay, in the golden sun, the lakes of the Atchafalaya.

Water-lilies in myriads rocked on the slight undulations

Made by the passing oars, and, resplendent in beauty, the lotus

Lifted her golden crown above the heads of the boatmen.

Faint was the air with the odorous breath of magnolia blossoms,

And with the heat of noon; and numberless sylvan islands,

Fragrant and thickly embowered with blossoming hedges of roses,

Near to whose shores they glided along, invited to slumber.

Soon by the fairest of these their weary oars were suspended.

Under the boughs of Wachita willows, that grew by the margin,

Henry Wadsworth Longfellow

The memorial church at Grand-Pré National Park,
Nova Scotia.

Photo: Sherman Hines

The Acadian communities that grew up around the
Bay of Fundy based their agriculture on reclaimed
marshland. Dykes held back the highest tides from
the upper reaches of the saltmarsh and permitted the
cultivation of large areas of wheat.

*When in the harvest heat she bore to the reapers
        at noontide
Flagons of home-brewed ale, ah! fair in sooth
        was the maiden*

Illustration: Frank Dicksee. From *Evangeline: the Place, the Story, the Poem*. Cassell, Petter, Galpin & Co., New York, 1882. In the collection of the Nova Scotia Legislative Library.

Meanwhile, apart, in the twilight gloom of a
window's embrasure,
Sat the lovers, and whispered together,
beholding the moonrise.

Fairest of all the maids was Evangeline,
    Benedict's daughter!
Noblest of all the youths was Gabriel,
    son of the blacksmith!

Still from the motion picture *Evangeline: A Romance of Acadia* (1920).

*Vain was the hope of escape; and cries and
    fierce imprecations
Rang through the house of prayer...*

Illustration: Jesse Wilcox Smith. From *Evangeline*. Houghton Mifflin and Company, Boston, 1897. In the collection of the Nova Scotia Legislative Library.

Came from the neighbouring hamlets and farms
the Acadian women,
Driving in ponderous wains their household
goods to the seashore.

Illustration: Frank Dicksee. From *Evangeline: the Place, the Story, the Poem*. Cassell, Petter, Galpin & Co., New York, 1882. In the collection of the Nova Scotia Legislative Library.

"Gabriel! be of good cheer! for if we love one
      another,
Nothing, in truth, can harm us, whatever mischances
      may happen!"

*And, as a signal sound, if others like them
        peradventure
Sailed on those gloomy and mignight streams,
        blew a blast on his bugle.*

Illustration: F. O. C. Darley. From *Evangeline*. Houghton Mifflin and Company, Boston, 1866. In the collection of the Nova Scotia Legislative Library.

Sometimes they saw, or thought they saw, the smoke of his camp-fire

Illustration: F. O. C. Darley. From *Evangeline*. Houghton Mifflin and Company, Boston, 1893. In the collection of the Nova Scotia Legislative Library.

Vainly he strove to rise; and Evangeline,
*   kneeling beside him,*
Kissed his dying lips, and laid his head
*   on her bosom.*

Illustration: Jane E. Bentham. From *Evangeline*. David Bogue
Publisher, London, 1850. In the collection of the Nova Scotia
Legislative Library.

Safely their boat was moored; and scattered about on the
greensward,

Tired with their midnight toil, the weary travellers slumbered.

Over them vast and high extended the cope of a cedar.

Swinging from its great arms, the trumpet-flower and the
grape-vine

Hung their ladder of ropes aloft like the ladder of Jacob,

On whose pendulous stairs the angels ascending, descending,

Were the swift humming-birds, that flitted from blossom to
blossom.

Such was the vision Evangeline saw as she slumbered
beneath it.

Filled was her heart with love, and the dawn of an opening
heaven

Lighted her soul in sleep with the glory of regions celestial.

*

Nearer and ever nearer, among the numberless islands,

Darted a light, swift boat, that sped away o'er the water,

Urged on its course by the sinewy arms of hunters and
trappers.

Northward its prow was turned, to the land of the bison and
beaver.

At the helm sat a youth, with countenance thoughtful and
careworn.

Dark and neglected locks overshadowed his brow, and a
sadness

Somewhat beyond his years on his face was legibly written.

Gabriel was it, who, weary with waiting, unhappy and restless,

Sought in the Western wilds oblivion of self and of sorrow.

Swiftly they glided along, close under the lee of the island,

But by the opposite bank, and behind a screen of palmettos,

So that they saw not the boat, where it lay concealed in the willows,

All undisturbed by the dash of their oars, and unseen, were the sleepers;

Angel of God was there none to awaken the slumbering maiden.

Swiftly they glided away, like the shade of a cloud on the prairie.

After the sound of their oars on the tholes had died in the distance,

As from a magic trance the sleepers awoke, and the maiden

Said with a sigh to the friendly priest,—"O Father Felician!

Something says in my heart that near me Gabriel wanders.

Is it a foolish dream, an idle and vague superstition?

Or has an angel passed, and revealed the truth to my spirit?"

Then, with a blush, she added,—"Alas for my credulous fancy!

Unto ears like thine such words as these have no meaning."

But made answer the reverend man, and he smiled as he answered,—

"Daughter, thy words are not idle; nor are they to me without meaning.

Feeling is deep and still; and the word that floats on the surface

Is as the tossing buoy, that betrays where the anchor is hidden.

Therefore trust to thy heart, and to what the world calls illusions.

Gabriel truly is near thee; for not far away to the southward,

On the banks of the Têche, are the towns of St. Maur and St. Martin.

There the long-wandering bride shall be given again to her
    bridegroom,
There the long-absent pastor regain his flock and his
    sheepfold.
Beautiful is the land, with its prairies and forests of fruit-trees;
Under the feet a garden of flowers, and the bluest of heavens
Bending above, and resting its dome on the walls of the forest.
They who dwell there have named it the Eden of Louisiana."

*

And with these words of cheer they arose and continued their
    journey.
Softly the evening came. The sun from the western horizon
Like a magician extended his golden wand o'er the
    landscape;
Twinkling vapors arose; and sky and water and forest
Seemed all on fire at the touch, and melted and mingled
    together.
Hanging between two skies, a cloud with edges of silver,
Floated the boat, with its dripping oars, on the motionless
    water.
Filled was Evangeline's heart with inexpressible sweetness.
Touched by the magic spell, the sacred fountains of feeling
Glowed with the light of love, as the skies and waters around
    her.
Then from a neighbouring thicket the mockingbird, wildest
    of singers,
Swinging aloft on a willow spray that hung o'er the water,
Shook from his little throat such floods of delirious music,
That the whole air and the woods and the waves seemed
    silent to listen.

Plaintive at first were the tones and sad; then soaring to
  madness

Seemed they to follow or guide the revel of frenzied
  Bacchantes.

Single notes were then heard, in sorrowful, low lamentation;

Till, having gathered them all, he flung them abroad in
  derision,

As when, after a storm, a gust of wind through the tree-tops

Shakes down the rattling rain in a crystal shower on the
  branches.

With such a prelude as this, and hearts that throbbed with
  emotion,

Slowly they entered the Têche, where it flows through the
  green Opelousas,

And through the amber air, above the crest of the woodland,

Saw the column of smoke that arose from a neighbouring
  dwelling;—

Sounds of a horn they heard, and the distant lowing of cattle.

III

Near to the bank of the river, o'ershadowed by oaks, from
  whose branches

Garlands of Spanish moss and of mystic mistletoe flaunted,

Such as the Druids cut down with golden hatchets at Yule-
  tide,

Stood, secluded and still, the house of the herdsman. A
  garden

Girded it round about with a belt of luxuriant blossoms,

Filling the air with fragrance. The house itself was of timbers
Hewn from the cypress-tree, and carefully fitted together.
Large and low was the roof; and on slender columns
   supported,
Rose-wreathed, vine-encircled, a broad and spacious veranda,
Haunt of the humming-bird and the bee, extended around it.
At each end of the house, amid the flowers of the garden,
Stationed the dove-cots were, as love's perpetual symbol,
Scenes of endless wooing, and endless contentions of rivals.
Silence reigned o'er the place. The line of shadow and
   sunshine
Ran near the tops of the trees; but the house itself was in
   shadow,
And from its chimney-top, ascending and slowly expanding
Into the evening air, a thin blue column of smoke rose.
In the rear of the house, from the garden gate, ran a pathway
Through the great groves of oak to the skirts of the limitless
   prairie,
Into whose sea of flowers the sun was slowly descending.
Full in his track of light, like ships with shadowy canvas
Hanging loose from their spars in a motionless calm in the
   tropics,
Stood a cluster of cotton-trees, with tangled cordage of grape-
   vines.

*

Just where the woodlands met the flowery surf of the prairie,
Mounted upon his horse, with Spanish saddle and stirrups,
Sat a herdsman, arrayed in gaiters and doublet of deerskin.
Broad and brown was the face that from under the Spanish
   sombrero

51

Gazed on the peaceful scene, with the lordly look of its
master.

Round about him were numberless herds of kine, that were
grazing

Quietly in the meadows, and breathing the vapory freshness

That uprose from the river, and spread itself over the
landscape.

Slowly lifting the horn that hung at his side, and expanding

Fully his broad, deep chest, he blew a blast, that resounded

Wildly and sweet and far, through the still damp air of the
evening.

Suddenly out of the grass the long white horns of the cattle

Rose like flakes of foam on the adverse currents of ocean.

Silent a moment they gazed, then bellowing rushed o'er the
prairie,

And the whole mass became a cloud, a shade in the distance.

Then, as the herdsman turned to the house, through the gate
of the garden

Saw he the forms of the priest and the maiden advancing to
meet him.

Suddenly down from his horse he sprang in amazement, and
forward

Rushed with extended arms and exclamations of wonder;

When they beheld his face, they recognized Basil the
Blacksmith.

Hearty his welcome was, as he led his guests to the garden.

There in an arbour of roses with endless question and answer

Gave they vent to their hearts, and renewed their friendly
embraces,

Laughing and weeping by turns, or sitting silent and
thoughtful.

Thoughtful, for Gabriel came not; and now dark doubts and
  misgivings

Stole o'er the maiden's heart; and Basil, somewhat
  embarrassed,

Broke the silence and said,—"If you came by the Atchafalaya,

How have you nowhere encountered my Gabriel's boat on the
  bayous?"

Over Evangeline's face at the words of Basil a shade passed.

Tears came into her eyes, and she said with a tremulous
  accent,

"Gone? is Gabriel gone?" and, concealing her face on his
  shoulder,

All her o'erburdened heart gave way, and she wept and
  lamented.

Then the good Basil said,—and his voice grew blithe as he
  said it,—

"Be of good cheer, my child; it is only to-day he departed.

Foolish boy! he has left me alone with my herds and my
  horses.

Moody and restless grown, and tried and troubled, his spirit

Could no longer endure the calm of this quiet existence.

Thinking ever of thee, uncertain and sorrowful ever,

Ever silent, or speaking only of thee and his troubles,

He at length had become so tedious to men and to maidens,

Tedious even to me, that at length I bethought me, and sent
  him

Unto the town of Adayes to trade for mules with the
  Spaniards.

Thence he will follow the Indian trails to the Ozark
  Mountains,

Hunting for furs in the forests, on rivers trapping the beaver.

Therefore be of good cheer; we will follow the fugitive lover;

He is not far on his way, and the Fates and the streams are against him.

Up and away to-morrow, and through the red dew of the morning

We will follow him fast, and bring him back to his prison."

*

Then glad voices were heard, and up from the banks of the river,

Borne aloft on his comrades' arms, came Michael the fiddler.

Long under Basil's roof had he lived like a god on Olympus,

Having no other care than dispensing music to mortals.

Far renowned was he for his silver locks and his fiddle.

"Long live Michael," they cried, "our brave Acadian minstrel!"

As they bore him aloft in triumphal procession; and straightway

Father Felician advanced with Evangeline, greeting the old man

Kindly and oft, and recalling the past, while Basil, enraptured,

Hailed with hilarious joy his old companions and gossips,

Laughing loud and long, and embracing mothers and daughters.

Much they marvelled to see the wealth of the ci-devant blacksmith,

All his domains and his herds, and his patriarchal demeanour;

Much they marvelled to hear his tales of the soil and the climate,

And of the prairies, whose numberless herds were his who would take them;

Each one thought in his heart, that he, too, would go and do likewise.

Thus they ascended the steps, and, crossing the breezy veranda,

Entered the hall of the house, where already the supper of Basil

Waited his late return; and they rested and feasted together.

*

Over the joyous feast the sudden darkness descended.

All was silent without, and, illuming the landscape with silver,

Fair rose the dewy moon and the myriad stars; but within doors,

Brighter than these, shone the faces of friends in the glimmering lamplight.

Then from his station aloft, at the head of the table, the herdsman

Poured forth his heart and his wine together in endless profusion.

Lighting his pipe, that was filled with sweet Natchitoches tobacco,

Thus he spake to his guests, who listened, and smiled as they listened:—

"Welcome once more, my friends, who so long have been friendless and homeless,

Welcome once more to a home, that is better perchance than the old one!

Here no hungry winter congeals our blood like the rivers;

Here no stony ground provokes the wrath of the farmer.

Smoothly the ploughshare runs through the soil, as a keel through the water.

All the year round the orange-groves are in blossom; and grass
grows
More in a single night than a whole Canadian summer.
Here, too, numberless herds run wild and unclaimed in the
prairies;
Here, too, lands may be had for the asking, and forests of
timber
With a few blows of the axe are hewn and framed into houses.
After your houses are built, and your fields are yellow with
harvests,
No King George of England shall drive you away from your
homesteads,
Burning your dwellings and barns, and stealing your farms
and your cattle."
Speaking these words, he blew a wrathful cloud from his
nostrils,
While his huge, brawny hand came thundering down on the
table,
So that the guests all started; and Father Felician, astounded,
Suddenly paused, with a pinch of snuff half-way to his
nostrils.
But the brave Basil resumed, and his words were milder and
gayer:—
"Only beware of the fever, my friends, beware of the fever!
For it is not like that of our cold Acadian climate,
Cured by wearing a spider hung round one's neck in a
nutshell!"
Then there were voices heard at the door, and footsteps
approaching
Sounded upon the stairs and the floor of the breezy veranda.
It was the neighbouring Creoles and small Acadian planters,

Who had been summoned all to the house of Basil the
    Herdsman.
Merry the meeting was of ancient comrades and neighbours:
Friend clasped friend in his arms; and they who before were
    as strangers,
Meeting in exile, became straightway as friends to each other,
Drawn by the gentle bond of a common country together.
But in the neighbouring hall a strain of music, proceeding
From the accordant strings of Michael's melodious fiddle,
Broke up all further speech. Away, like children delighted,
All things forgotten beside, they gave themselves to the
    maddening
Whirl of the dizzy dance, as it swept and swayed to the music,
Dreamlike, with beaming eyes and the rush of fluttering
    garments.

*

Meanwhile, apart, at the head of the hall, the priest and the
    herdsman
Sat, conversing together of past and present and future;
While Evangeline stood like one entranced, for within her
Olden memories rose, and loud in the midst of the music
Heard she the sound of the sea, and an irrepressible sadness
Came o'er her heart, and unseen she stole forth into the
    garden.
Beautiful was the night. Behind the black wall of the forest,
Tipping its summit with silver, arose the moon. On the river
Fell here and there through the branches a tremulous gleam
    of the moonlight,
Like the sweet thoughts of love on a darkened and devious
    spirit.

Nearer and round about her, the manifold flowers of the
garden

Poured out their souls in odors, that were their prayers and
confessions

Unto the night, as it went its way, like a silent Carthusian.

Fuller of fragrance than they, and as heavy with shadows and
night-dews,

Hung the heart of the maiden. The calm and the magical
moonlight

Seemed to inundate her soul with indefinable longings,

As, through the garden gate, and beneath the brown shade of
the oak-trees,

Passed she along the path to the edge of the measureless
prairie.

Silent it lay, with a silvery haze upon it, and fire-flies

Gleaming and floating away in mingled and infinite numbers.

Over her head the stars, the thoughts of God in the heavens,

Shone on the eyes of man, who had ceased to marvel and
worship,

Save when a blazing comet was seen on the walls of that
temple,

As if a hand had appeared and written upon them, "Upharsin."

And the soul of the maiden, between the stars and the fire-
flies,

Wandered alone, and she cried,—"O Gabriel! O my beloved!

Art thou so near unto me, and yet I cannot behold thee?

Art thou so near unto me, and yet thy voice does not reach
me?

Ah! how often thy feet have trod this path to the prairie!

Ah! how often thine eyes have looked on the woodlands
around me!

Ah! how often beneath this oak, returning from labor,

Thou hast lain down to rest, and to dream of me in thy
slumbers!

When shall these eyes behold, these arms be folded about
thee?"

Loud and sudden and near the note of a whippoorwill
sounded

Like a flute in the woods; and anon, through the
neighbouring thickets,

Farther and farther away it floated and dropped into silence.

"Patience!" whispered the oaks from oracular caverns of
darkness;

And, from the moonlit meadow, a sigh responded, "To-
morrow!"

*

Bright rose the sun next day; and all the flowers of the garden

Bathed his shining feet with their tears, and anointed his
tresses

With the delicious balm that they bore in their vases of crystal.

"Farewell!" said the priest, as he stood at the shadowy
threshold;

"See that you bring back the Prodigal Son from his fasting
and famine;

And, too, the Foolish Virgin, who slept when the bridegroom
was coming."

"Farewell!" answered the maiden, and, smiling, with Basil
descended

Down to the river's brink, where the boatmen already were
waiting.

Thus beginning their journey with morning, and sunshine,
and gladness,

Swiftly they followed the flight of him who was speeding
    before them,

Blown by the blast of fate like a dead leaf over the desert.

Not that day, nor the next, nor yet the day that succeeded,

Found they the trace of his course, in lake or forest or river,

Nor, after many days, had they found him; but vague and
    uncertain

Rumors alone were their guides through a wild and desolate
    country;

Till, at the little inn of the Spanish town of Adayes,

Weary and worn, they alighted, and learned from the
    garrulous landlord,

That on the day before, with horses and guides and
    companions,

Gabriel left the village, and took the road of the prairies.

IV

Far in the West there lies a desert land, where the
    mountains

Lift, through perpetual snows, their lofty and luminous
    summits.

Down from their desolate, deep ravines, where the gorge, like
    a gateway,

Opens a passage rude to the wheels of the emigrant's wagon,

Westward the Oregon flows and the Walleway and Owyhee.

Eastward, with devious course, among the Windriver
    mountains,

Through the Sweet-water Valley precipitate leaps the Nebraska;

And to the south, from Fontaine-qui-bout and the Spanish sierras,

Fretted with sands and rocks, and swept by the wind of the desert,

Numberless torrents, with ceaseless sound, descend to the ocean,

Like the great chords of a harp, in loud and solemn vibrations.

Spreading between these streams are the wondrous, beautiful prairies,

Billowy bays of grass ever rolling in shadow and sunshine,

Bright with luxuriant clusters of roses and purple amorphas.

Over them wandered the buffalo herds, and the elk and the roebuck;

Over them wandered the wolves, and herds of riderless horses;

Fires that blast and blight, and winds that are weary with travel;

Over them wander the scattered tribes of Ishmael's children,

Staining the desert with blood; and above their terrible war-trails

Circles and sails aloft, on pinions majestic, the vulture,

Like the implacable soul of a chieftain slaughtered in battle,

By invisible stairs ascending and scaling the heavens.

Here and there rise smokes from the camps of these savage marauders;

Here and there rise groves from the margins of swift-running rivers;

And the grim, taciturn bear, the anchorite monk of the desert,

Climbs down their dark ravines to dig for roots by the brook-
side;
And over all is the sky, the clear and crystalline heaven,
Like the protecting hand of God inverted above them.

*

Into this wonderful land, at the base of the Ozark Mountains,
Gabriel far had entered, with hunters and trappers behind
him.
Day after day, with their Indian guides, the maiden and Basil
Followed his flying steps, and thought each day to o'ertake
him.
Sometimes they saw, or thought they saw, the smoke of his
camp-fire
Rise in the morning air from the distant plain; but at nightfall,
When they had reached the place, they found only embers
and ashes.
And, though their hearts were sad at times and their bodies
were weary,
Hope still guided them on, as the magic Fata Morgana
Showed them her lakes of light, that retreated and vanished
before them.

*

Once, as they sat by their evening fire, there silently entered
Into the little camp an Indian woman, whose features
Wore deep traces of sorrow, and patience as great as her
sorrow.
She was a Shawnee woman returning home to her people,
From the far-off hunting-grounds of the cruel Camanches,
Where her Canadian husband, a Coureur-de-Bois, had been
murdered.

Touched were their hearts at her story, and warmest and
    friendliest welcome

Gave they, with words of cheer, and she sat and feasted
    among them

On the buffalo-meat and the venison cooked on the embers.

But when their meal was done, and Basil and all his
    companions,

Worn with the long day's march and the chase of the deer and
    the bison,

Stretched themselves on the ground, and slept where the
    quivering fire-light

Flashed on their swarthy cheeks, and their forms wrapped up
    in their blankets,

Then at the door of Evangeline's tent she sat and repeated

Slowly, with soft, low voice, and the charm of her Indian
    accent,

All the tale of her love, with its pleasures, and pains, and
    reverses.

Much Evangeline wept at the tale, and to know that another

Hapless heart like her own had loved and had been
    disappointed.

Moved to the depths of her soul by pity and woman's
    compassion,

Yet in her sorrow pleased that one who had suffered was near
    her,

She in turn related her love and all its disasters.

Mute with wonder the Shawnee sat, and when she had
    ended

Still was mute; but at length, as if a mysterious horror

Passed through her brain, she spake, and repeated the tale
    of the Mowis;

Mowis, the bridegroom of snow, who won and wedded a
maiden,

But, when the morning came, arose and passed from the
wigwam,

Fading and melting away and dissolving into the sunshine,

Till she beheld him no more, though she followed far into the
forest.

Then, in those sweet, low tones, that seemed like a weird
incantation,

Told she the tale of the fair Lilinau, who was wooed by a
phantom,

That, through the pines o'er her father's lodge, in the hush of
the twilight,

Breathed like the evening wind, and whispered love to the
maiden,

Till she followed his green and waving plume through the
forest,

And never more returned, nor was seen again by her people.

Silent with wonder and strange surprise, Evangeline listened

To the soft flow of her magical words, till the region around
her

Seemed like enchanted ground, and her swarthy guest the
enchantress.

Slowly over the tops of the Ozark Mountains the moon rose,

Lighting the little tent, and with a mysterious splendor

Touching the sombre leaves, and embracing and filling the
woodland.

With a delicious sound the brook rushed by, and the branches.

Swayed and sighed overhead in scarcely audible whispers.

Filled with the thoughts of love was Evangeline's heart, but a
secret,

Subtile sense crept in of pain and indefinite terror,

As the cold, poisonous snake creeps into the nest of the
swallow.

It was no earthly fear. A breath from the region of spirits

Seemed to float in the air of night; and she felt for a moment

That, like the Indian maid, she, too, was pursuing a phantom.

And with this thought she slept, and the fear and the
phantom had vanished.

*

Early upon the morrow the march was resumed; and the
Shawnee

Said, as they journeyed along,—"On the western slope of
these mountains

Dwells in his little village the Black Robe chief of the
Mission.

Much he teaches the people, and tells them of Mary and
Jesus;

Loud laugh their hearts with joy, and weep with pain, as they
hear him."

Then, with a sudden and secret emotion, Evangeline
answered,—

"Let us go to the Mission, for there good tidings await us!"

Thither they turned their steeds; and behind a spur of the
mountains,

Just as the sun went down, they heard a murmur of voices,

And in a meadow green and broad, by the bank of a river,

Saw the tents of the Christians, the tents of the Jesuit
Mission.

Under a towering oak, that stood in the midst of the village,

Knelt the Black Robe chief with his children. A crucifix
fastened

High on the trunk of the tree, and overshadowed by grape-
vines,

Looked with its agonized face on the multitude kneeling
beneath it.

This was their rural chapel. Aloft, through the intricate arches

Of its aerial roof, arose the chant of their vespers,

Mingling its notes with the soft susurrus and sighs of the
branches.

Silent, with heads uncovered, the travellers, nearer
approaching,

Knelt on the swarded floor, and joined in the evening
devotions.

But when the service was done, and the benediction had
fallen

From the hands of the priest, like seed from the hands of the
sower,

Slowly the reverend man advanced to the strangers, and bade
them

Welcome; and when they replied, he smiled with benignant
expression,

Hearing the homelike sounds of his mother-tongue in the
forest,

And with words of kindness, conducted them into his
wigwam.

There upon mats and skins they reposed, and on cakes of the
maize-ear

Feasted, and slaked their thirst from the water-gourd of the
teacher.

Soon was their story told; and the priest with solemnity
answered:—

"Not six suns have risen and set since Gabriel, seated

On this mat by my side, where now the maiden reposes,

Told me this same sad tale; then arose and continued his
    journey!"

Soft was the voice of the priest, and he spake with an accent
    of kindness;

But on Evangeline's heart fell his words as in winter the
    snow-flakes

Fall into some lone nest from which the birds have departed.

"Far to the north he has gone," continued the priest; "but in
    autumn,

When the chase is done, will return again to the Mission."

Then Evangeline said, and her voice was meek and
    submissive—

"Let me remain with thee, for my soul is sad and afflicted."

So seemed it wise and well unto all; and betimes on the
    morrow,

Mounting his Mexican steed, with his Indian guides and
    companions,

Homeward Basil returned, and Evangeline stayed at the
    Mission.

*

Slowly, slowly, slowly the days succeeded each other,—

Days and weeks and months; and the fields of maize that
    were springing

Green from the ground when a stranger she came, now
    waving above her,

Lifted their slender shafts, with leaves interlacing, and forming

Cloisters for mendicant crows and granaries pillaged by
    squirrels.

Then in the golden weather the maize was husked, and the
    maidens

Blushed at each blood-red ear, for that betokened a lover,

But at the crooked laughed, and called it a thief in the corn-
field.

Even the blood-red ear to Evangeline brought not her lover.

"Patience!" the priest would say; "have faith, and thy prayer
will be answered!

Look at this delicate flower that lifts its head from the
meadow,

See how its leaves all point to the north, as true as the
magnet;

It is the compass flower, that the finger of God has suspended

Here on its fragile stalk, to direct the traveller's journey

Over the sea-like, pathless, limitless waste of the desert.

Such in the soul of man is faith. The blossoms of passion,

Gay and luxuriant flowers, are brighter and fuller of fragrance,

But they beguile us, and lead us astray, and their odor is
deadly.

Only this humble plant can guide us here, and hereafter

Crown us with asphodel flowers, that are wet with the dews of
nepenthe."

*

So came the autumn, and passed, and the winter,— yet
Gabriel came not;

Blossomed the opening spring, and the notes of the robin and
blue-bird

Sounded sweet upon wold and in wood, yet Gabriel came not.

But on the breath of the summer winds a rumor was wafted

Sweeter than song of bird, or hue or odor of blossom.

Far to the north and east, it said, in the Michigan forests,

Gabriel had his lodge by the banks of the Saginaw River.

And, with returning guides, that sought the lakes of St.
    Lawrence,
Saying a sad farewell, Evangeline went from the Mission.
When over weary ways, by long and perilous marches,
She had attained at length the depths of the Michigan forests,
Found she the hunter's lodge deserted and fallen to ruin!

*

Thus did the long sad years glide on, and in seasons and
    places
Divers and distant far was seen the wandering maiden;—
Now in the tents of grace of the meek Moravian Missions,
Now in the noisy camps and the battle-fields of the army,
Now in secluded hamlets, in towns and populous cities.
Like a phantom she came, and passed away unremembered.
Fair was she and young, when in hope began the long
    journey;
Faded was she and old, when in disappointment it ended.
Each succeeding year stole something away from her beauty,
Leaving behind it, broader and deeper, the gloom and the
    shadow.
Then there appeared and spread faint streaks of gray o'er her
    forehead,
Dawn of another life, that broke o'er her earthly horizon,
As in the eastern sky the first faint streaks of the morning.

V

In that delightful land which is washed by the Delaware's
    waters,

Guarding in sylvan shades the name of Penn the apostle,

Stands on the banks of its beautiful stream the city he
    founded.

There all the air is balm, and the peach is the emblem of
    beauty,

And the streets still re-echo the names of the trees of the
    forest,

As if they fain would appease the Dryads whose haunts they
    molested.

There from the troubled sea had Evangeline landed, an exile,

Finding among the children of Penn a home and a country.

There old René Leblanc had died; and when he departed,

Saw at his side only one of all his hundred descendants.

Something at least there was in the friendly streets of the city,

Something that spake to her heart, and made her no longer a
    stranger;

And her ear was pleased with the Thee and Thou of the
    Quakers,

For it recalled the past, the old Acadian country,

Where all men were equal, and all were brothers and sisters.

So, when the fruitless search, the disappointed endeavour,

Ended, to recommence no more upon earth, uncomplaining,

Thither, as leaves the light, were turned her thoughts and her
    footsteps.

As from a mountain's top the rainy mists of the morning

Roll away, and afar we behold the landscape below us,

Sun-illumined, with shining rivers and cities and hamlets,

So fell the mists from her mind, and she saw the world far
below her,

Dark no longer, but all illumined with love; and the pathway

Which she had climbed so far, lying smooth and fair in the
distance.

Gabriel was not forgotten. Within her heart was his image,

Clothed in the beauty of love and youth, as last she beheld
him,

Only more beautiful made by his deathlike silence and
absence.

Into her thoughts of him time entered not, for it was not.

Over him years had no power; he was not changed, but
transfigured;

He had become to her heart as one who is dead, and not
absent;

Patience and abnegation of self, and devotion to others,

This was the lesson a life of trial and sorrow had taught her.

So was her love diffused, but, like to some odorous spices,

Suffered no waste nor loss, though filling the air with aroma.

Other hope had she none, nor wish in life, but to follow

Meekly, with reverent steps, the sacred feet of her Saviour.

Thus many years she lived as a Sister of Mercy; frequenting

Lonely and wretched roofs in the crowded lanes of the city,

Where distress and want concealed themselves from the
sunlight,

Where disease and sorrow in garrets languished neglected.

Night after night, when the world was asleep, as the
watchman repeated

Loud, through the gusty streets, that all was well in the city,

High at some lonely window he saw the light of her taper.

Day after day, in the gray of the dawn, as slow through the suburbs

Plodded the German farmer, with flowers and fruits for the market,

Met he that meek, pale face, returning home from its watchings.

*

Then it came to pass that a pestilence fell on the city,

Presaged by wondrous signs, and mostly by flocks of wild pigeons,

Darkening the sun in their flight, with naught in their craws but an acorn.

And, as the tides of the sea arise in the month of September,

Flooding some silver stream, till it spreads to a lake in the meadow,

So death flooded life, and, o'erflowing its natural margin,

Spread to a brackish lake, the silver stream of existence.

Wealth had no power to bribe, nor beauty to charm, the oppressor;

But all perished alike beneath the scourge of his anger;—

Only, alas! the poor, who had neither friends nor attendants,

Crept away to die in the almshouse, home of the homeless.

Then in the suburbs it stood, in the midst of meadows and woodlands;—

Now the city surrounds it; but still, with its gateway and wicket

Meek, in the midst of splendor, its humble walls seem to echo

Softly the words of the Lord:—"The poor ye always have with you."

Thither, by night and by day, came the Sister of Mercy. The
dying
Looked up into her face, and thought, indeed, to behold there
Gleams of celestial light encircle her forehead with splendor,
Such as the artist paints o'er the brows of saints and apostles,
Or such as hangs by night o'er a city seen at a distance.
Unto their eyes it seemed the lamps of the city celestial,
Into whose shining gates ere long their spirits would enter.

*

Thus, on a Sabbath morn, through the streets, deserted and
silent,
Wending her quiet way, she entered the door of the
almshouse.
Sweet on the summer air was the odor of flowers in the
garden;
And she paused on her way to gather the fairest among them,
That the dying once more might rejoice in their fragrance and
beauty.
Then, as she mounted the stairs to the corridors, cooled by
the east wind,
Distant and soft on her ear fell the chimes from the belfry of
Christ Church,
And, intermingled with these, across the meadows were
wafted
Sounds of psalms, that were sung by the Swedes in their
church at Wicaco.
Soft as descending wings fell the calm of the hour on her
spirit;
Something within her said,—"At length thy trials are ended;"
And, with light in her looks, she entered the chambers of
sickness.

Noiselessly moved about the assiduous, careful attendants,

Moistening the feverish lip, and the aching brow, and in silence

Closing the sightless eyes of the dead, and concealing their faces,

Where on their pallets they lay, like drifts of snow by the road-side.

Many a languid head, upraised as Evangeline entered,

Turned on its pillow of pain to gaze while she passed, for her presence

Fell on their hearts like a ray of the sun on the walls of a prison.

And, as she looked around, she saw how Death, the consoler,

Laying his hand upon many a heart, had healed it for ever.

Many familiar forms had disappeared in the nighttime;

Vacant their places were, or filled already by strangers.

*

Suddenly, as if arrested by fear or a feeling of wonder,

Still she stood, with her colorless lips apart, while a shudder

Ran through her frame, and, forgotten, the flowerets dropped from her fingers,

And from her eyes and cheeks the light and bloom of the morning.

Then there escaped from her lips a cry of such terrible anguish,

That the dying heard it, and started up from their pillows.

On the pallet before her was stretched the form of an old man.

Long, and thin, and gray were the locks that shaded his temples;

But, as he lay in the morning light, his face for a moment
Seemed to assume once more the forms of its earlier manhood;
So are wont to be changed the faces of those who are dying.
Hot and red on his lips still burned the flush of the fever,
As if life, like the Hebrew, with blood had besprinkled its
    portals,
That the Angel of Death might see the sign, and pass over.
Motionless, senseless, dying, he lay, and his spirit exhausted
Seemed to be sinking down through infinite depths in the
    darkness,
Darkness of slumber and death, forever sinking and sinking.
Then through those realms of shade, in multiplied
    reverberations,
Heard he that cry of pain, and through the hush that
    succeeded
Whispered a gentle voice, in accents tender and saint-like,
"Gabriel! O my beloved!" and died away into silence.
Then he beheld, in a dream, once more the home of his
    childhood;
Green Acadian meadows, with sylvan rivers among them,
Village, and mountain, and woodlands; and, walking under
    their shadow,
As in the days of her youth, Evangeline rose in his vision.
Tears came into his eyes; and as slowly he lifted his eyelids,
Vanished the vision away, but Evangeline knelt by his
    bedside.
Vainly he strove to whisper her name, for the accents
    unuttered
Died on his lips, and their motion revealed what his tongue
    would have spoken.

Vainly he strove to rise; and Evangeline, kneeling beside him,
Kissed his dying lips, and laid his head on her bosom.
Sweet was the light of his eyes; but it suddenly sank into
    darkness,
As when a lamp is blown out by a gust of wind at a casement.

All was ended now, the hope, and the fear, and the sorrow,
All the aching of heart, the restless, unsatisfied longing,
All the dull, deep pain, and constant anguish of patience!
And, as she pressed once more the lifeless head to her bosom,
Meekly she bowed her own, and muttered, "Father, I thank
    Thee!"

✤ ✤ ✤

Still stands the forests primeval; but far away from its shadow,
Side by side, in their nameless graves, the lovers are sleeping.
Under the humble walls of the little Catholic church-yard,
In the heart of the city, they lie, unknown and unnoticed.
Daily the tides of life go ebbing and flowing beside them,
Thousands of throbbing hearts, where theirs are at rest and
    for ever,
Thousands of aching brains, where theirs no longer are busy,
Thousands of toiling hands, where theirs have ceased from
    their labors,
Thousands of weary feet, where theirs have completed their
    journey!

*

Still stands the forest primeval; but under the shade of its
    branches

Dwells another race, with other customs and language.

Only along the shore of the mournful and misty Atlantic

Linger a few Acadian peasants, whose fathers from exile

Wandered back to their native land to die in its bosom.

In the fisherman's cot the wheel and the loom are still busy;

Maidens still wear their Norman caps and their kirtles of homespun,

And by the evening fire repeat Evangeline's story,

While from its rocky caverns the deep-voiced, neighbouring ocean

Speaks, and in accents disconsolate answers the wail of the forest.